GRUNT

Ad Minorem Gloriam Porcorum

and to MARY BREWER *and* DAVID FELSEN

who taught me everything I've forgotten

———————————

LIBRARY OF CONGRESS CATALOGING-IN-PUBLICATION DATA
BOYNTON, SANDRA
GRUNT: PIGORIAN CHANT FROM SNOUTO DOMOINKO DE SILO
WRITTEN, COMPOSED AND ILLUSTRATED BY SANDRA BOYNTON.
P. CM.   ISBN 0-7611-0594-8 (ALK. PAPER)
1. CHANTS (PLAIN, GREGORIAN, ETC.)—HUMOR.
2. WIT AND HUMOR, MUSICAL. 3. ANIMALS—HUMOR.
I. TITLE
ML65.B68 1996
782.2'92'0207—DC20   96-32265 CIP MN

WORKMAN PUBLISHING COMPANY, INC., 708 BROADWAY, NEW YORK, NY 10003-9555

MANUFACTURED IN MEXICO
FIRST PRINTING: OCTOBER 1996
10 9 8 7 6

Pigorian Chant

from SNOUTO DOMOINKO DE SILO

GRUNT

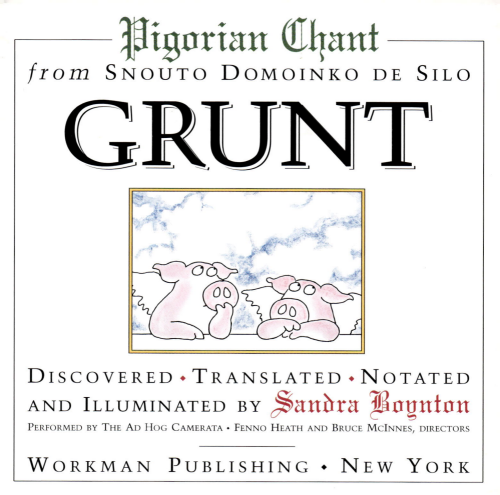

DISCOVERED · TRANSLATED · NOTATED
AND ILLUMINATED BY Sandra Boynton

PERFORMED BY THE AD HOG CAMERATA · FENNO HEATH AND BRUCE MCINNES, DIRECTORS

WORKMAN PUBLISHING · NEW YORK

DAYBREAK AT SNOUTO DOMOINKO DE SILO

Introduction

SNUGGLED IN AN OVERGROWN VALLEY outside an obscure town in a remote corner of an insignificant country on a forgotten continent is the non-existent farmstead of Snouto Domoinko de Silo. Here, for many many centuries, the pleasingly obeisant Domoinkan Pigs have lived humbly and quietly. Well okay, not entirely quietly. Twelve times a day, every day of the year, rain or shine, like it or not, the simple swine of Snouto Domoinko grunt the unadorned, ethereal music of Pigorian Chant. And here, for those same many many centuries, other creatures of lesser spiritual depth have responded as best they can to the resonating chants.

The origins of Pigchant are obscure, but scholars tell us that it dates back to before the time of Caesar Hogustus. The world has all but forgotten this, our oldest music. Yet in their ancient and echoing stone grange, the murmuring Domoinkan Pigs still calmly contemplate the Meaning of Things in their well-worn mystical and quasi-musical way.

As they have been for, again, many many centuries, the Pigs are called thrice daily from their peaceful slumbers or from their melodic meditations to bow their unworldly heads and sup at their ancient stone trough:

"Sooee. Sooo-ee."

It is the impatient farmer. The Pigs pause in their solemn unison singing, or stir in their solemn unison snoring, and listen:

"SOOOOOOOOOOOOOOOOOOOO-EEEE."

Shifting almost imperceptibly from the Chant of Repose (the hypnotic *Ore-snay, Ore-snay*) or the Chant of Reflection (the profoundly inquisitive *Y-whay Are-ay E-way Ere-hay?*) into the Chant of Sublime Anticipation (the inspiring *Op-slay Ime-tay*), the humble Pigs trot serenely across the cobbled courtyard to the place of food.

Should a small band of weary tourists happen upon this place that Time has snubbed, they might, as they crest the overlooking hill, hear rising toward them the mystical strains of some strange, simple, timeless, compelling, epiphanic, beautiful, possibly lucrative music. They pause. They listen…

Surely, it must be the Pigs.

If these same wanderers happen to have about them a dozen or so SX-iq87 Nikito full-spectrum microphones with Xetron pre-amps hooked up to a 24-track CDAT synchronizer backed up by a Series G Coventry console nestled in a trailerful of generators, they could perhaps be fortunate enough to capture this unpretentious music, to share with other seekers in the hectic modern world beyond.

Different listeners find different resonances in Pigchant. Some hear Humility. Some hear Yearning. Some hear Infinite Peace. Some hear Effortless Ecstasy Beyond All Striving. Some hear Solace, Reassurance, and Hope. Some few visionaries have discerned Opportunity.

Here, then, is the essential music of the Domoinkan Pigs—and the earnest chanted responses of their brethren and sistern cows, chickens, sheep, and ducks—carried reverently across the oceans, across the centuries, from the simple farm of Snouto Domoinko into your jacuzzi. Whenever you feel vaguely disgruntled, whenever you sense that you have somehow lost your way, listen again to this timeless music, to reaffirm that life offers renewal. To be suffused with the eternity of Eternity. To understand that there is always a second *Chants*.

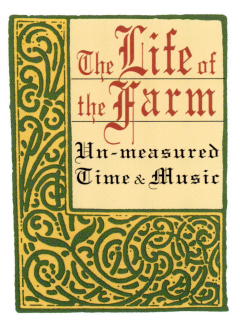

The Life of the Farm

Un-measured Time & Music

THE NOTION OF TIME as we most commonly understand it is quite different from swine time: Tempus Porco Nihil Est ("Time to a pig means zilch"), as the laconic cows observe in the *Vis Inertiae*. For the Pigs of Snouto Domoinko de Silo, the day unfolds according to an intrinsic rhythm of mood and purpose, rather than to the measured units of a clock.

Each of the twelve events of the Pigs' day is heralded by the tolling of a gently irksome bell; each has its own particular accompanying Pigchant—evocative, unadorned, strictly modal unison chant, intoned in the traditional Pig Latin. The interspersed exhortations of the weary farmer are similarly plain, though here the text is in ordinary Latin.

The responsive chant and interjectories of the lesser barnyard animals, in Latin also, are less austere, less calmly inexorable. Though still primarily in unison, the voices do here and there diverge, creating an unearthly blend in counterpoint to the steadfast porkers. It should also be noted that the optimistic chickens sing exclusively in two- and three-part polyphony. It was most likely this phenomenon that led Julius Caesar to observe: *Omnes Gallinae in partes tres divisae sunt* ("All chickens are divided into three parts").

Between their unhurried meditations and their sincere meals, the contemplative Pigs emerge at random intervals from the stone walls and vaulted ceilings of their ancient stone grange, to calmly consider the sun, gratefully receive the air, or joyfully extemporize in the mud. Or perhaps they venture outside for the traditional *Iffing-snay Out-ay Acks-snay*. And during the long afternoons, the Pigs close their eyes, slow their breathing, and—apparently oblivious to the implorings of their more worldly fellow beings—intone once again the unremitting triads of the *Ore-snay, Ore-snay*.

The evensong follows the third troughtime of the day. Here it is not primarily the Pigs, but the other animals that carry the diurnal journey to its peaceful close. Vespers is a hushed tonal dialogue of closure, a responsory chant of the various farm animals urging sleep in unhurried measures of quiet persuasion, though perhaps it should be admitted that the cows have just about had it by this time.

The essence of farm life is somewhat different for the animals of each zoological order, depending on their intrinsic natures. For the amiable Pigs, it is a life of contemplation, sustenance, and repose; for the enigmatic cows, a life of skeptical rumination; for the complacent sheep, a life of conformity and shear patience; for the garrulous chickens, a life of expressive eggstacy. Yet for all, there is great comfort to be drawn from the predictable monotony of each day. From the predawn snoring of the Pigs to their melismatic midmorn musings to the cows' lowing *Allemooia*s to evensong's counting of the sheep to the ultimate lingering chicken *Pax*, an ineffable calm descends.

Listen. It is an experience like no other.

S.K. BOYNTON, PY.G.
Ad Hog Historian

The Chants

Monophonia Noctis

Monophony of the Night

PIGS:

Ore-snay. Ore-snay.
Ore-snay. Ore-snay.
Ore-snay. Ore-snay.

Snore, snore,
snore, snore,
snore, snore…

I. Anima Fundi

1. Life-Breath of the Farm

[BELL TOLLS FOUR]

i. Spiritus

i. Spirit

VOICE:

Vox spiritus fundi
sumus.
Dormiunt omnes.
Stertunt Porci clari.
Auscultate:

We are the voice
of the spirit of the farm.
Everyone is asleep.
The famous Pigs are snoring.
Listen:

PIGS:

Ore-snay. Ore-snay.
Ore-snay. Ore-snay.
Ore-snay. Ore-snay.

Snore, snore,
snore, snore,
snore, snore…

ii. Aurora
[BELL TOLLS FIVE]

ROOSTER:
Coccadoodul du.
Ego dixi:
Coccadoodul du.

CHICKENS:
O, primam lucem.
Sol surgit.
Gallus magnifice
incedens exclamat.
Nunc venit agricola.

SOLO CHICKEN:
Ecce Macdonaldus Senex,
qui fundum habet.
E-I-E-I-O.

COWS:
Et in hoc fundo,
nonnullas boves
domesticas habet.
E-I-E-I-O.
Cum moo moo hic,
cum moo moo ibi.

ii. Dawn

Cock-a-doodle-doo.
I said,
Cock-a-doodle-doo.

O, first light!
The sun is rising.
The strutting
rooster calls.
Now comes the farmer.

Behold Old MacDonald,
who has a farm.
E I E I O.

And on this farm,
he has
some cows.
E I E I O.
With a moo moo here,
and a moo moo there.

Hic una moo,	*Here a moo,*
ibi una moo,	*there a moo,*
ubique una moo moo.	*everywhere a moo moo.*

SOLO CHICKEN:

Macdonaldus Senex	*Old MacDonald*
fundum habet.	*has a farm.*
E-I-E-I-O.	*E I E I O.*
Et in hoc fundo,	*And on this farm,*
nonnullos porcos	*he has some pigs.*
habet. E-I-E-I-O.	*E I E I O.*

DUX:

Ni oink oink hic.	*No oink oink here.*
Ni oink oink ibi.	*No oink oink there.*
Ubi sunt Porci	*So where are the Pigs*
quoquomodo?	*already?*

FARMER:

Sooo-ee. Sooooooo-eeee.	*Sooee, sooee.*
Ubi sunt Porci quoquomodo?	*So where are the Pigs already?*

CHICKENS:

Dormiunt.	*They're sleeping.*
Vocat ad se frustra.	*He summons in vain.*

FARMER:

Et in Arcadia sum.	*And **this** is pastoral paradise?*

II. Prima Vocatio

[BELL TOLLS ONE]

FARMER:
Porcos cibumque cano.
Venite, Porci.
Soooo-ee. Soooooooooooo-eee.

PIGS:
Et-lay us-ay eep-slay.
Ease-play et-lay us-ay eep-slay.

CHICKENS:
Consurgite, Porci.
Sol fulget. Dies serenus est.
Dicimus: Consurgite, Porci.

FARMER:
Sol fulgat. Dies serenus est.

PIGS:
Et-lay us-ay eep-slay.
Ease-play et-lay us-ay eep-slay.

FARMER:
O, Porci ignavissimi. Ignavissimi.
Sooooooooo-eee.

PIGS' RESPONSE:
Ooooooo, no-oooo way.

2. First Call

I sing of pigs and the food.
Come, Pigs!
Sooee, sooee.

Let us sleep.
Please let us sleep.

Get up, Pigs!
The sun shines. It's a lovely day.
We said, Get up, Pigs!

Let the sun shine! It's a lovely day.

Let us sleep.
Please let us sleep.

Oh, you lazy, lazy, lazy Pigs!
Sooee.

Ooh. No way.

III. Vocatio Secunda
[BELL TOLLS TWO]

3. Second Call

FARMER:
Soooo-ee. Soooooooooo-eee.
Si non nunc
venietis,
cibum gallinis
dabo.

Sooee, sooee.

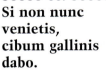

If you don't
come now,
I'll give your food
to the chickens.

CHICKENS:
Sententia bona.

Good idea!

PIGS' RESPONSE:
Op-stay, op-stay.
E're-way oming-cay.

Stop, stop,
we're coming!

IV. Jejunium Fractum
[BELL TOLLS THREE]

4. Breaking the Fast

PIGS:
Op-slay ime-tay. Op-slay ime-tay.
Op-slay ime-tay. Op-slay ime-tay.
Ood-fay, orious-glay ood-fay.
Um-yay, um-yay.

Slop time! Slop time!
Slop time! Slop time!
Food, glorious food!
Yum yum.

COWS:
Mirabile visu.

That's an astounding sight.

V. Cogitatio in Horreo
[BELL TOLLS FOUR]

5. Meditation in the Barn

CHICKENS:
Demum veniunt Porci.

At last, here come the Pigs.

SOLO CHICKEN:
**Pleni sunt Porci,
et sollemnes.**

*The Pigs are full,
and solemn.*

CHICKENS:
**Brevi audiemus
canticum sonorum
profundumque.
Auscultate:**

*Soon we will hear
their song, sonorous
and profound.
Listen:*

PIGS:
**Y-whay are-ay
e-way ere-hay?
Y-whay are-ay
e-way ere-hay?
E-way are-ay ere-hay o-tay ing-say
in-ay ig-Pay atin-Lay
ome-say ery-vay erious-say
usic-may.
Isten-lay.
Ote-nay e-thay ervading-pay**

*Why are
we here?
Why are
we here?
We are here to sing
in Pig Latin
some very serious
music.
Listen.
Note the pervading*

ense-say of-ay alm-cay	*sense of calm*
and-ay ystery-may.	*and mystery.*
At-whay is-ay e-thay eaning-may	*What is the meaning*
of-ay ife-Lay?	*of Life?*
At-whay is-ay e-thay eaning-may	*What is the meaning*
of-ay eaning-May?	*of Meaning?*
E-way o-day ot-nay ow-knay.	*We do not know.*
Ut-bay ow-nay it-ay is-ay	*But now it is*
e-thay ickens'-chay urn-tay	*the chickens' turn*
o-tay ing-say.	*to sing.*

CHICKENS:

Cantate canticum pro nobis.	*Sing a song for us.*

PIGS:

Pro vobis.	*For you.*

CHICKENS:

Ovum apparuit.	*An egg appeared.*
Multitudo ovorum apparuit.	*A multitude of eggs appeared.*
Non sequitur.	*It does not follow.*
Gloria in eggshells	*Glory in eggshells*
each day-o.	*each day. O.*
Gloria in eggshells	*Glory in eggshells*
each day-o.	*each day. O.*

COWS:

Quisque comoedus est.	*Everybody's a comedian.*

PIGS:

Ank-thay ou-yay, ickens-chay.	*Thank you, Chickens.*
And-ay ow-nay e-way urmur-may	*And now we murmur*
once-(w)ay ore-may is-thay	*once more this*
umble-hay	*humble*
elodic-may ine-lay.	*melodic line.*
Ut-bay ow-nay it-ay is-ay	*But now it is*
e-thay eep's-shay urn-tay.	*the sheep's turn.*

SHEEP:

Oves et agni sumus	*We are sheep and lambs,*
qui sequuntur quemlibet.	*who follow anyone.*
Quo vadis?	*Whither goest thou?*
Illuc venimus etiam.	*We go thither, too.*
Quid exspectatis?	*So what do you expect?*
Oves et agni sumus	*We are sheep and lambs,*
qui cantant,	*who are singing,*
cantant Baaaaaaaa-aaaaa.	*singing 'Baaa.'*

PIGS:

Y-whay are-ay e-way ere-hay?
E-way are-ay ere-hay
o-tay ing-say
ad nauseam
ome-say ery-vay erious-say
usic-may.
Ut-bay ow-nay it-ay is-ay
e-thay ows'-cay urn-tay.

Why are we here?
We are here
to sing
relentlessly
some very serious
music.
But now it is
the cows' turn.

COWS:

Margaritas ante porcos.
Allemooia, allemooooooooia.
Tantum est.

Pearls before swine.
Allemooia, allemooia.
That's all.

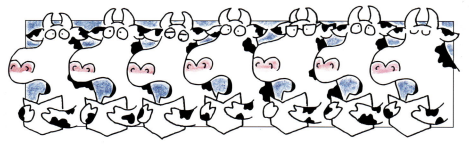

CHICKENS:

Altissima quaeque flumina
minimo sono fluunt.

The deepest rivers flow
with the least sound.

VI. Exsultatio in Campo   6. Frolic in the Field
[BELL TOLLS TWO]

PIGS:

E-thay ucks-day are-ay alling-cay.
Isten-lay.
Ack-quay, ack-quay.
At-whay are-ay ey-thay ying-tray
o-tay ell-tay us-ay?

The ducks are calling.
Listen:
"Quack, quack."
What are they trying
to tell us?

DUX:

Venite, venite.
Cadit pluvia,
terra
inundatur.
Venite, gaudeamus.
Quaqua. Quaqua.
Quaqua.

Come on out!
The rain is falling,
the ground
is all soggy.
Come on, let's party.
Any way. Any way.
Any way.

PIGS:

Ud-may, ondrous-way ud-may.
Ook-lay out-ay,
ere-hay e-way ome-cay.

Mud, wondrous mud!
Look out,
here we come!

DUX:

Quaqua. Quaqua. Quaqua.   *Any way. Any way. Any way.*

COWS:
Detestamur pluviam.   *We hate the rain.*

SHEEP:
Pariter.   *Likewise.*

CHICKENS:
Pariter.   *Likewise.*

VII. **Meridies**   7. Noon
[BELL TOLLS TWELVE]

FARMER:
Hora prandi est.   *It's lunchtime.*
Venite, Porci.   *Come, Pigs!*
O, soooo-eee. Sooooooooo-eeeee.   *Oh, sooee, sooee.*

PIGS:
Op-slay ime-tay. Op-slay ime-tay.   *Slop time! Slop time!*
Op-slay ime-tay. Op-slay ime-tay.   *Slop time! Slop time!*
Ood-fay, orious-glay ood-fay.   *Food, glorious food!*
Um-yay, um-yay.   *Yum yum.*

COWS:
Mirabile visu.   *That's an astonishing sight.*

VIII. 𝕭𝖗𝖊𝖇𝖎𝖘 𝕾𝖔𝖒𝖓𝖚𝖘   8. Naptime

i. [BELL TOLLS ONE]

PIGS:

Ime-tay or-fay our-ay ap-nay.   *Time for our nap.*
Ore-snay. Ore-snay.   *Snore, snore,*
Ore-snay. Ore-snay.   *snore, snore,*
Ore-snay. Ore-snay.   *snore, snore…*

ii. [BELL TOLLS TWO]

CHICKENS:

Consurgite, Porci.   *Piggies, arise!*
Diem absumitis.   *You are wasting the day.*

PIGS:

Ore-snay. Ore-snay.   *…snore, snore,*
Ore-snay. Ore-snay.   *snore, snore,*
Ore-snay. Ore-snay.   *snore, snore…*

iii. [BELL TOLLS THREE]

CHICKENS:

Consurgite, Porci.   *Piggies, arise!*
Diem absumitis.   *You are wasting the day.*

PIGS:
Ore-snay. Ore-snay.
Ore-snay. Ore-snay.
Ore-snay. Ore-snay.

…snore, snore,
snore, snore,
snore, snore…

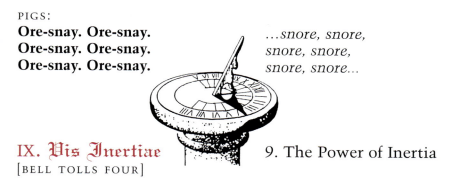

IX. Vis Inertiae
[BELL TOLLS FOUR]

9. The Power of Inertia

CHICKENS:
Consurgite, Porci.
Sol occidit.

Piggies, arise!
The sun is setting.

SOLO CHICKEN:
Diem absumitis.

You are wasting the day.

PIGS:
Et-lay us-ay eep-slay.
Ease-play et-lay us-ay eep-slay.

Let us sleep.
Please let us sleep.

CHICKENS:
Consurgite, Porci.
Carpite diem.
Consurgite, Porci.

Piggies, arise!
Seize the day!
Piggies, arise!

PIGS:
Et-lay us-ay eep-slay.
Ease-play et-lay us-ay eep-slay.

Let us sleep.
Please let us sleep.

SHEEP:
O, Porci ignavissimi.
Hora fugit.

Oh, you lazy Piggies.
The hour escapes.

COWS:
Tempus porco nihil est.

What's time to a hog?

CHICKENS:
Consurgite, Porci.

Piggies, arise!

PIGS' RESPONSE:
Ooooooo, no-oooo way.

Ooh. No way.

X. Investigatio Tuberibus

[BELL TOLLS FIVE]

PIG OF EXPERIENCE:
Ake-way up-ay, uys-gay.
E-thay ain-ray as-hay oppèd-stay.
E-way an-cay unt-hay
or-fay uffles-tray
in-ay e-thay oods-way.

RESPONSE:
Id-day ou-yay ay-say
uffles-tray?
At-whay are-ay e-way
aiting-way or-fay?

COWS:
De gustibus
non est disputandum.

10. The Search for Truffles

Wake up, guys!
The rain has stopped!
We can hunt
for truffles
in the woods!

Did you say
TRUFFLES?
What are we
waiting for?

There's no accounting
for taste.

XI. Epulae Tales Quales Sunt
[BELL TOLLS SĬX]

11. A Feast, Such As It Is

FARMER:
Hora cenae est.
Venite, Porci.
O, soo-ee.
Sooooooooooo-eee.

It's dinner time.
Come, Pigs.
Oh, sooee.
Sooee.

PIGS:
Op-slay ime-tay.
Op-slay ime-tay.
Op-slay ime-tay.
Op-slay ime-tay.
Ood-fay,
orious-glay ood-fay.
Um-yay, um-yay.

Slop time!
Slop time!
Slop time!
Slop time!
Food,
glorious food!
Yum yum.

COWS:
Mirabile visu.

That's an astonishing sight.

XII. Nox Animalium Nobilium

[BELL TOLLS ONE]

FARMER:
Tempus dormitum ire est.

SHEEP:
Oves et agni sumus.
Numerate nos:
Unus. Duo. Tres.

12. Night of the Noble Beasts

It's time to go to sleep.

We are sheep and lambs.
Count us.
One, two, three...

PIGS:
E-way are-ay o-say ired-tay.
Awwwwwn-yay.
Ood-gay ight-nay.

We are so tired.
Yawn.
Good night.

SHEEP:

Oves et agni sumus.
Numerate nos:
Quattuor. Quinque.
Sex. Septem.

We are sheep and lambs.
Count us.
Four, five,
six, seven...

COWS:

Mooo-oo-ooo-oo-ooo.

Mooooo.

SHEEP:

O, oves et agni sumus.
Numerate nos:
Octo. Novem. Decem.

Oh, we are sheep and lambs.
Count us.
Eight, nine, ten...

DUX:

Quaqua. Quaqua.
Quaqua. Quaqua.

Whatever.

PIGS:
Et-lay us-ay eep-slay.
Ease-play et-lay us-ay eep-slay.

Let us sleep.
Please let us sleep.

SHEEP:
Undecim. Duodecim.
Tredecim.

…eleven, twelve,
thirteen…

CHICKENS:
In saecula saeculorum.

For ever and ever.

COWS:
Cacoëthes loquendi.

Compulsive talking.

SHEEP:
Quattuordecim. Quindecim.
Sedecim.

…fourteen, fifteen,
sixteen…

COWS:
Et in Arcadia sumus.

Country life is overrated.

CHICKENS:
Noctem bonam.

Good night.

COWS:
Pacem. Pacem.

Shhhhhhhh.

CHICKENS:
Valete ac plaudite.

Farewell, and applaud.

COWS:
Non plaudite.
Modo pecuniam jacite.

Don't applaud,
just throw money.

CHICKENS:
Sententia bona.

Good idea.

PIGS:
Ore-snay. Ore-snay.
Ore-snay. Ore-snay.
Ore-snay. Ore-snay.

ZZZZZZZZZZZZ
ZZZZZZZZZZZZ
ZZZZZZZZZZZZ...

COWS:
Tantum est.

That's all.

SOLO CHICKEN:
Sufficit.

It's more than enough.

𝕍𝕖𝕣𝕓𝕦𝕞 𝕌𝕝𝕥𝕚𝕞𝕦𝕞

[BELL TOLLS EIGHT]

The Last Word

CHICKENS:
Pax.

Peace.

SNOUTO DOMOINKO DE SILO SLEEPS

Credits & Acknowledgments

PERFORMED BY
The Ad Hog Camerata
UNDER THE DIRECTION OF
FENNO HEATH & BRUCE McINNES

VOX SPIRITUS FUNDI: THE HEATHS
ROOSTER: DAVID CLEVELAND
SOLO CHICKEN: LUCY HEATH McLELLAN
FARMER: MARK DOLLHOPF
PIG OF EXPERIENCE: FENNO HEATH

CHICKENS, DUCKS, SHEEP:
> JUDITH BOYNTON
> EMILY BLAIR CHEWNING
> SARAH HEATH
> LUCY HEATH McLELLAN
> PEGGY HEATH OGILVY
> ROSALYN PEACHEY
> LYNNE RUFF
> KATHLEEN TORRANT SHERRILL

PIGS, SHEEP, COWS:
> MARK CAPECELATRO
> TIMOTHY DeWERFF
> MARK DOLLHOPF
> MICHAEL FORD
> TIM HAWKINS
> FENNO HEATH III (TERRY)
> ROBERTO IFILL
> ROBERT JENSEN
> BRUCE McINNES
> GEORGE YOUNGER

WORDS AND MUSIC: SANDRA BOYNTON
LATIN EDITOR: BOB SOHRWEIDE
> *THE HOTCHKISS SCHOOL CLASSICS DEPARTMENT*
COMPOSITION CONSULTANT: FENNO HEATH
> *DIRECTOR OF THE YALE GLEE CLUB EMERITUS*
PERFORMANCE ADVISOR: BRUCE McINNES
> *CHOIRMASTER, GRACE CHURCH*

BOOK EDITOR: SUZANNE RAFER
BOOK DESIGN: SANDRA BOYNTON
> *and* PAUL HANSON
PRODUCTION: WAYNE KIRN

RECORDING PRODUCED BY
Sandra Boynton

ASSISTANTS: SARAH HEATH, KATHLEEN SHERRILL
RECORDING ENGINEER: DEVIN EMKE
ASSISTANT ENGINEER: ZACK WIND
> *SOUND ON SOUND (NYC)*
MASTERING ENGINEER: HENK KOOISTRA
> *9 WEST (MARLBOROUGH, MA)*

AND A SINCERE Gratias TO:
> BARBARALYNN ALTORFER, JEANNE BOYNTON,
> ROBERT BOYNTON, JUDITH CALDWELL,
> JANE CAPECELATRO, MICHAEL FORD, DAVE KUTCH,
> KYLE PRUETT, MATTHEW RINGEL,
> ANN SELZNICK, JOANNE SOHRWEIDE

*And, as always, oink you very much to Jamie, Caitlin,
and Devin McEwan and Keith and Darcy Boynton*